Behold, I stand at the door, and knock: if any man hear my voice, and open the door, I will come in to him, and will sup with him, and him with me
-Revelations 3:20

Depths

of

the Soul

Poetry From Within

Margaret White

Copyright © 2020 by Margaret White.

Depths of the Soul
Poetry From Within
by Margaret White

Printed in the United States of America

ISBN 978-1-7347266-1-9

All rights reserved solely by the author. No part of this book may be altered, copied, photographed, tampered with in any manner whatsoever. No part of this book may be used or reproduced without written permission by the author Margaret White

Scripture quotations taken from the King James Version. (KJV)-public domain

****Acknowledgments****

God has always been there for me through every difficult time in my life and he has brought me through, every single time, for this he is the greatest impact on my life

Bishop Randy and Pastor Gayle Brown you are acknowledged for the big heart that both of you possess. All the prays that were and are being prayed I am truly thankful

I acknowledge Eddie and Jessica Backus for the time spent with me to pour into the vision that God has given. Jessica thank you for the knowledge that you have shared with me which caused this book to come forth. I thank God for placing such gifts in my Life

Pastor John Norris you are acknowledged for pushing me to do greater things even at my difficult time when I didn't see the greater

Yvonne Mann you are acknowledged for not giving up on me and helping me to get to my goals in life

Ryan Munoz my son you are acknowledged because even though you are busy you always find time to help me thank you son

Patricia Shirley you have sowed so much wisdom, knowledge and time into me, I appreciate and love you very much for being there and encouraging me. and for being my friend

My sister Marie Carmant for being a excellent sister to me and always being there

Also Sister Vera Davis , Sister Juanita Jackson, and Sister Michelle Mills for being awesome church sisters

I would like to also acknowledge Shashika Idushan she is the one who assisted with the enhancement of the cover for my book. She did an amazing job. She is on Fiverr.com

All of you have been a blessing to me and I totally appreciate all of your help, all of you were definitely God sent and I am thankful

Introduction

Depths of the Soul are inspirational poems that will cause you to search within yourself and to explore the depths of your soul. Many times we have questions left unanswered which pertain to ourselves. These poems will cause you to open up an area in your life that has not been examined. This book will cause you to desire a deeper relationship with God and cause you to want to get closer to Him. So, as you read these poems, I encourage you to follow these simple steps as you read each of these poems.

READ, STOP, READ, then LISTEN

All poems inspired by God through his Holy Spirit

God Is Able

Encouraging Words

For God so loved the world, that he gave his only begotten Son, that whosoever believeth in him should not perish, but have everlasting life
John 3:16

That if thou shalt confess with thy mouth the Lord Jesus, and shalt believe in thine heart that God hath raised him from the dead, thou shalt be saved   Romans 10:9

For whosoever shall call upon the name of the Lord shall be saved   Romans 10:13

Are You Ready?

Depths of the Soul
"Poetry From Within"

Table of Contents

Poem Title	Page
All Things	2
Anger	6
Beautiful	10
Decisions	14
Destination	18
Expectation	22
Instructions	26
Power	30
Purpose	34
Questions	38
Still Small Voice	42
Stranger	46
Trust	50
Vision	54
Weapons	58
Who Is That Voice	62
Wondering	66
Destined	70

Dive Into
the Depths of the Soul

"All Things"

All things were made by him, but no one knows who he is

He created us from the dust of the earth, but no one knows who he is

When we need help he always comes to the rescue, but no one knows who he is

When we feel alone we feel him calling, but no one knows who he is

He remains a mystery to many, because no one knows who he is

He sent his Son Jesus Christ to die for us, but no one knows who he is

He gave us a second chance, but no one knows who he is

He continues to call us, but we are never home, because no one knows who he is

He loves us so much, but we do not love him, because no one knows who he is

He gave his all so that we can come back to him, but no one knows who he is

He left instructions for us to get to him, but no one knows who he is

Time is running out and we are on our way to hell, but no one knows who he is

One day we will stand before him, and he will say I never knew who you were

What Did You Hear God Say To You?

"Anger"

Anger is dangerous

It blinds you, and causes you not to see

Anger is a device that is used to destroy

It should not be looked at, as a toy

Destroy the vision, the purpose ,and all you strive to be

Anger is a trap if you do not know you will see

It is a plan to bring you down low

When anger comes, you must quickly make it go

By releasing the anger that you hold

As quickly as it comes is as quickly as it should go

But people just do not know

Anger leads to other doors

Such as wrath, rage and much, much more

God said be angry but sin not

That is the way you stay on top

On top of all situations and circumstances

But you must trust God

Trust God to set you free

Deliverance is the key, to unlock your destiny

The key to unlock all your bondages

And all the mess, but first you must pass the test

Be angry but sin not

What Did You Hear God Say To You?

"Beautiful"

In time he makes all things beautiful, if you wait on him

Your life may be upside down, but in his time, he will make things beautiful

Sometimes we do not like the way we look, but God says your beautiful

We have a lot of worries, but in time, he makes things beautiful

We may say, I do not know if I can make it, but, in his time, he will give you the strength

All things that come from God are beautiful including his Son Jesus Christ

The path that we walk is not clear, but God wants to lead the way and make things beautiful

But if we trust in and believe in God he will fix

all things and make them beautiful

We look at the flowers and how beautiful they

are, it took time to get them that way, God makes things beautiful

Just like it will take time to make you into the person that he has called you to be, God will make things beautiful

He takes his time because he is not in a rush, because God is into perfection and God makes things beautiful

There will be a time that you will see the person that God has called you too be and you are beautiful

If you wait on him, and let him do it in his time it will be beautiful

What Did You Hear God Say To You?

"Decisions"

A decision must be made where you will go

Because of sin, hell is where you were meant to go

Only you can change your path

But if you do not, you will be a part of Gods' wrath

God has given us a way out of hell

But the devil has cast his spell

God has moved the lies for you so that you may know the truth

Jesus died so you may have life and have life more abundantly

And God has given you sight to see, that the change must be made

But only you can choose this day

Choose life over death, choose blessing over curses, the choice is yours

But know this, the decision must be made, time is running out, and Jesus is willing to pay the price for your soul

So make a decision to go to heaven or stay on the road to destruction which is your original call because of sin

                    Choose life today

What Did You Hear God Say To You?

"Destination"

When I was born, my destination was hell
Why you may ask because of sin
All day long sin presented itself to me, and every day I fell
Fell for the same trap that is taking me to hell
Sin is a trap to keep you on the wrong path
Sin makes itself look so good
One day I was so fed up with the lies of this world
Then someone came and told me about a man that brought me victory long ago, his name is Jesus
Since then, I have been hooked, and I will not leave this man that died for me on cavalry
I now have a choice and I have made up my mind

Now I am saved from the pit of hell, and now I was sent to tell, the good news of the word of God, that the devil can only go but so far, and that he is defeated

The decision is yours, but you must pick, its either the penthouse or the pit

The truth or the devils lies and tricks

The devil is there to fool you, if you allow him too

He is not your friend, he is out to destroy you but Jesus came to set you free, he is with you until the end, and Jesus is your victory

Heaven is where I want to be how about you

What Did You Hear God Say To You?

_____

_____

_____

_____

_____

_____

_____

_____

_____

_____

"Expectation"

As I wait in expectation

For the promises of God to manifest

The devil constantly testes my faith

Even though I said the sinners pray and I am no longer in bondage with him

The devil continues to try to pull me back in

But I must stand strong and see the salvation of the Lord

For God is good and worthy of praise

The troubles of the world are not my concern, they are Gods'

For God said in his word, to cast all your cares on him and this is what I do

In all I do, I must put my trust in him

For God is faithful in all his ways

He will teach me, and lead me through this path that the world has given

I am no longer the same, for God has transformed me into a new creature; that is created in his image

No longer will sin have a hold on me

I have decided to follow Gods' ways internally

No matter what the trial, no matter what the test may be

I Wait in Expectation

What Did You Hear God Say To You?

"Instructions"

Instructions and directions has been left, but no wants to follow

People say they do not know the way, but no one wants to follow

He left instructions for us, to know how to get to him, but no one wants to follow

They say its too hard to follow Gods' way, because no one wants to follow

In the time of need they inquire about the instructions, but no one wants to follow

Many are called but few are chosen because no one wants to follow

The devil is out to kill, steal and destroy, but no one wants to follow

The world is on its way to judgment, but no

one wants to follow

They say they love him, but their hearts are far from him, because no one wants to follow

There will be a time when you will be asked did you follow my instructions

Many will say, I did not know the way, but God will say you did not want to follow

What Did You Hear God Say To You?

"Power"

Power is given when you give your life; give your life to who you may say

Give your life to the person that has been waiting for you God our Heavenly Father

Power is given when sacrifice is made, sacrifice to who you may say

To the one that made you and gave you breath, the Almighty and living God
Sacrifice is required to fulfill this call, sacrifice what you may say
Sacrifice your time, sacrifice your life, and sacrifice your all
All power was given, when Jesus gave his life, he gave his all so that we may have life

We must give our life to get what Jesus got, what did he get you may ask

All wisdom, all power, all strength, and Gods' all

That is the exchange that Jesus made for us all

The power is optional because the price must be paid

The price is sacrifices are you willing to pay

Jesus did it all when he gave his life, now we must continue to pay the price

Pay the price to stay set free; to continue to have the victory

Accept now before it is too late, when it comes to God he is never late

Come to him and let him clean your slate and make the adjustments necessary in his time

What Did You Hear God Say To You?

"Purpose"

What is my purpose? I know now

My purpose is the vision that God has laid out for my life

God has created me with purpose

Purpose to fulfill his desires and his plans

Even though I do not know the fullness of Gods' will I know in my heart that I can trust him

Who is he? The one that created me the one that placed me in my mothers womb

He is God the Almighty One, counselor, comforter, the great I am he is God

There is more to me that meets the eye, but only God can reveal the secrets, the lies that I hide inside

The devil has placed things in me that was meant to destroy me

But God came to save me and now I see

He can place me on the road to victory, if I accept his hand I see

The road I was on was a road to destruction

But I have made up my mind to choose life over death

My true purpose is revealed; revealed day by day, as I pray

My purpose has changed, and God knows what is best for me

 I do have a purpose on this earth; it is to serve God with all my heart, mind and soul

God does not create anything without purpose

What Did You Hear God Say To You?

"Questions"

Questions enter my mind everyday

But answers I do not have

Who is this man named Jesus, that died on cavalry for me

I know I need to ask more questions

To lead me to the right way

I know change must take place

And I wonder will I have the courage

To make up my mind

That heaven is where I want to go

Many questions, little answers

But God knows it all

Maybe when I answer his call

My answers will begin to flow

I know its God I need

I know I need to be set free

So, I have come to a conclusion

That God has all the answers

Not myself, not the world, not nothing but God

God awaits your questions because He sure has the answers

What Did You Hear God Say To You?

"Still Small Voice"

There is a still, small voice

That talks to me, and wants to lead me

But day by day I am too busy or lazy

In the night I sit still, and I hear

A still, small voice calling me

I ask myself is it me

But I know its not, because I do not live free

My life is going so fast at times, I can not control it

I need help to be put on the right track

Part of me knows I need to be free

Free from sin, free from bondage free from everything

Constantly I hear a still, small voice

Talking to me, but the enemy constantly traps me

I know which way I need to go

But the devil will not loosen his hold

What I need to do is listen

There is a still, small voice

Trying to point the way, but the question is

        Will You Obey

What Did You Hear God Say To You?

"Stranger"

There is a stranger in my life, that knew me before I was born

This stranger constantly tries to gain a relationship with me

But I always run away, where ever I go the stranger is there

This stranger constantly calls me, but I am never there

I only acknowledge him in my time of need

I do not know why this stranger picked me

There are so many other people out there, but it seems like he knows me

I begin to wonder should I answer the call

Every time I hear this strangers voice in my heart

A part of me wants to call out to Him

But I do not know how, to trust someone I cannot see

I know I need this stranger in my life

The question is am I willing to let Him in and let Him change me

What Did You Hear God Say To You?

"Trusting"

Trusting is hard when you cannot see who
you're putting your all into
Trusting means to rely on, rely on God
God tells us to trust in him with all our heart
We must trust even though we don't know
Know what to expect, but know it's only a test
that we take
Trusting God when we don't know
Know what his plans are but he knows
Knows the plans and knows the reasons
Why we go through these trials and tests
God is there, you must know
The important thing is that you don't let go
We run, we hide because we don't trust
But trusting is a serious thing
Trusting sometimes causes you to sing

Sing unto God because you know

That he loves, and he cares about you

Trusting is not as easy as it seems

It takes time and effort to work it in

God is calling because he wants you to trust

Trust in him and his promises

But repentance is the key to righteousness

So will you trust in the only one that knows your destiny

TRUST

What Did You Hear God Say To You?

"Vision"

When God created me, I had a vision

But then sin came and made it blurry

I could not see what God had for me

My life was empty, and I was blind

To the fact where I was losing my mind

But God came and restored my sight and filled my life

With his vision and his life

Now through Jesus a new vision has been given to me and now I have something hold on to.

Constantly the devil tries to steal that vision that God has given me,

But I will fight with my weapon which is prayer and the Word of God

Many weapons we own such as praise, prayer, dance and much more

To keep the vision that has been placed in me

Through the Holy Spirit is how God leads

And I am determined not to lose Gods' vision for my life so that I may succeed

        I will follow Gods' vision for my life

What Did You Hear God Say To You?

"Weapons"

In this world we were taught how to fight

We were lied to and taught that the only way to fight is with guns and knives

But what we were not taught was that there are greater and stronger weapons not of this world

These mighty and strong weapons are prayer, and the Word of God

We are accustom to fighting in the natural but we were never taught how to fight in the spiritual realm

The natural way never solves the problem

But in the spiritual realm you go to the root of the problem

The Word of God says for our weapons are not carnal

which we were taught, but mighty through God

which goes straight to the root

Guns and knives are not the key, but prayer and faith brings the keys

Guns and knives will not solve our issues

But the Word of God will solve all things

When you open your mouth and say

God can you make a way

God will fix all things

What Did You Hear God Say To You?

"Who is that Voice"

There are times we feel depressed

Then you hear a voice say it will be ok.

There are times that you feel angry

And you hear a voice say let it go

There are times you feel that you can not go on

Then you hear a voice say hold on help is on the way

There are times you feel lonely

And you hear a voice say your not alone

There are times you feel afraid

Then you hear, God has not given you a spirit of fear

You may sit and ask, who is that voice

That voice is God calling you closer to him

Will you open your heart, and let him in?

Will you trade your life of sin?

For joy, peace, love, hope, and strength

Jesus said he is the way the truth and the life
God stands at the door and knocks
He wants to know when you will open the
door instead of locking it
The door to your heart, the door to your life
Who is that voice speaking
It is God in your mist

What Did You Hear God Say To You?

_____

_____

_____

_____

_____

_____

_____

_____

_____

_____

"Wondering"

We spend our lives wondering

If there is a heaven or a hell

We see things happen before us

And wonder, is there a heaven or a hell

We feel a tug on our heart

And we wonder if there is a heaven or a hell

We feel torn inside between good and evil

And we wonder is there a heaven or a hell

We spend our lives wondering is God real

But the day our lives end, will determine

If there is a heaven and if there is a hell

Peoples lives are destroyed daily

And we still wonder is there a heaven and a hell

We know we need God, but we have our stubborn way.

We prefer to keep wondering
Is there a heaven and a hell

Instead of seeking God

Wondering, wondering, wondering is that you

Will you put down the pride and search for the truth.

    Wondering, wondering, wondering

What Did You Hear God Say To You?

"Destined"

From the day that God placed you in your mothers womb you were chosen by Him to do a great work. God has been calling you for a very long time; now is the opportunity to answer him. As you have been reading these poems God has been speaking to you. God is giving you an opportunity to reunite with him. The sins in your life have separated you from Him and he does not hear your prayer. Isaiah 59:2 but your iniquities have separated you from your God and your sins have hid his face from you that he will not hear. If you felt a tug on your heart, or you had to stop and think about what you were reading, then God is trying to get your attention; and now that he has it, he wants you to know that he loves you. But the decision is yours. If you decide that you want a relationship with God again then repeat this sinners prayer. We are all sinners and God wants to save us. Think about it. Is your life that good that it is worth going to hell for?

What profit a man if he gain the whole world and lose his soul.... Mark 8:36 also in Hebrews 9:27 it states and as it is appointed unto men once to die, but after this the judgment. The decision is yours and the keys are in your hand now, which is this prayer of salvation. God is not in your life right now in Revelations 3:20 it says behold I stand at the door and knock; if any man hear my voice I will come in and sup with him and he with me. If you want God in your life say this prayer.

Prayer of Salvation

God I am a sinner and I admit that I have done wrong. I come to you for forgiveness and want to say I am sorry for all the wrong I have done. I believe that you sent your Son Jesus Christ to die for my sins, and I am willing to turn away from sin and follow you. Lead me and guide me to your path of righteousness in Jesus name. I now invite Jesus Christ into my heart and my life as my personal Lord and Savior. Thank you for salvation. I am now saved in Jesus name. Congratulations on the best decision that you have made in your life.

My prayer for you is:

God, I ask that you keep them and order their steps. I ask that you direct them in the way that you have for them. I ask that your will be done in their lives and that you will teach them your ways. I ask that the seed that was planted continue to be watered and you bring the increase. I ask that every chain, shackle and stronghold be broken off their lives right now in Jesus name. I ask that you send them to the church home that you have for them and let them continue to grow in your word and your truth. Satan, I bind you off of their lives right now in Jesus name I bind the spirit of oppression, and depression, lying and deceiving spirits, doubt and unbelief in Jesus name. I bind the spirit of fear in the name of Jesus.

I bind the spirit of spiritual and natural death in Jesus name. I bind all addictions, lust, and pride in Jesus name. I Loose humility, Gods' will to be done in your life, boldness, peace,

liberty, joy, Gods love, truth, and strength in Jesus name.
Be blessed and find a church home

Notes:

Date that you said the sinner's prayer and got saved:_____

_____

Which poem(s) spoke to you the most?

_____

_____

_____

Thoughts:

_____

_____

_____

Always Remember
Jesus did it all for you
The True Love of God

Jesus Christ
gave it all up for you

About the Author

Margaret White is a five-fold Evangelist that has a strong passion and a desire for souls to be saved. She wants the same passion that is within her to spread throughout the Body of Christ while evangelizing. She is expecting for more laborers to join the kingdom of God so that there will be more laborers going out into the harvest.

The passion that Margaret White has is so hearty that she has committed to teach, train and equip the Body of Christ by imparting the five-fold evangelistic anointing ,by the leading of the Holy Spirit.

She desires to see Gods' will done on earth as it is in heaven, and to have more laborers step into their calling and to fulfill the call on their life. She also desires to be used by God in a mighty way to activate the laborer so that they can experience a personal and a outward revival within the Body of Christ so that the harvest will be tended to.

Margaret White has held several Evangelism Courses to stir up the passion within the believer to go out and evangelize. She has also held Evangelism Team training Courses to develop Evangelism teams so that souls will be saved properly and added to the kingdom of God. She has organized evangelism teams to win souls for Christ which included street and train (subway) evangelism. She held classes to develop the gifts within the Body of Christ. The goal of these trainings are to equip the army of God to go out and reap precious souls for Christ and to begin individual revival within the Body of Christ.

She has been sent by God to deposit the Evangelistic Anointing within the Body of Christ and to those that believe on Jesus Christ by training those in the Body of Christ effectively and to have signs following. She has also implemented and assisted in various evangelistic crusade efforts.

She has visited various churches to teach her courses and during her trainings those that attended her classes and course has come back with multiple testimonies during and after these training.

These trainings have made a huge impact in the Body of Christ and have affected the unbeliever and cause them to come to Christ through the Word of God that has come forth from these teachings.

Margaret White is a dedicated wife and she is a mother to 4 wonderful children Ryan Munoz, Jeremiah White, Ceana White, and Adonya White. She is a determined servant of God and proud to be.

Thank you for reading my book, I pray that it blessed you.

   May God Bless You and Keep You in Jesus name.

Jesus is calling
you.
Will you answer
the call?

The choice
is yours